The Laughing Monkeys
Of Gravity

□

The Laughing Monkeys
Of Gravity

□

□

□

Stephen Bluestone

□

Mercer · 1995

□

ISBN 0-86554-452-2

The Laughing Monkeys of Gravity

by Stephen Bluestone

Copyright © 1995
Mercer University Press, Macon, Georgia 31207 USA

The paper used in this publication meets the minimum
requirements of the American National Standard for Information
Sciences—Permanence of Paper for Printed Library Materials,
ANSI Z39.48-1984.

Library of Congress Cataloging-in-Publication Data

Bluestone, Stephen.
The Laughing Monkeys of Gravity/ Stephen Bluestone
    viii + 63 pp.   6x9"
    ISBN 0-86554-452-2
    I. Title.
    PS3552.L815L38   1994   94-27079
    811'. 54—dc20   CIP

CONTENTS

I. Landscapes and Seasons

II. A Vaudeville of the Heart

III. Songs and Voices

ACKNOWLEDGEMENTS

Many of the poems in this collection, some in earlier form, first appeared in the following periodicals: *Brandeis Review*, "Speaking of Cousins"; *Cumberland Poetry Review*, "Three Anatomists"; *The Greensboro Review*, "First Voices," "A Circumstance of the Porch," and "Bewildering Clarity of Tongues"; *Israel Horizons*, "Lord Elgin's Marbles"; *Midstream*, "Singing" and "Moses Maimonides"; *Poetry*, "The Unveiling"; *The Sewanee Review*, "A Garland for Skelton" and "Saint Bernard of Clairvaux"; *Southern Poetry Review*, "In a Cemetery of the Bialystok District"; *The Sow's Ear*, "The Laughing Monkeys of Gravity."

"First Voices" won *The Greensboro Review*'s Poetry Prize, and "Three Anatomists" was a second-place winner in the *Cumberland Poetry Review*'s Robert Penn Warren Poetry Competition.

I wish to express grateful appreciation to the following for the assistance that made this book possible: the Georgia Arts Council for an Individual Artist Fellowship and the Office of the Dean of the College of Liberal Arts, Mercer University, for development grants. Personal thanks to Joyce Dykes, Donald Hall, Tom Huber, and Jon Peede for their help and friendship.

Cover art: Harold Lloyd in *Safety Last*. Courtesy of the Academy of Motion Picture Arts and Science.

for Keiren

I. Landscapes and Seasons

*"So! I have climbed high, and my reward
is small. Here I stand, with wearied knees,
earth, indeed, at a dizzy depth below, but
heaven far, far beyond me still."*
> —Nathaniel Hawthorne

*"The scenery was extremely picturesque,
and notwithstanding our forlorn condition,
we were frequently obliged to stop and admire it."*
> —John C. Fremont

THE UNVEILING

Now the world's only
season's growing older,
the low stubble
of the shuttling sky
and night, too,
a blanket of conclusions.

Of course, we could also say:
When night comes,
whatever's in the ground
will keep like a new year
in winter's closet,
and, sooner or later, it, too,
will make ghosts of all
brief distinctions.

And add:
That these dead kin
are not so perfectly dead
as not to be somehow in motion,
somehow stored up in us,
their other limbs and faces,
here in the light.

But they were great
talkers once, themselves;
now they're as finished as the world is,
and done with listening, too.

What can we say about them,
having known them
as we cannot know the world?
What can we say about them now,
to keep them as kin?

Something should be said.
Now's the time to say something,
if we ever will,
about the differences
between love and the world.

LORD ELGIN'S MARBLES

We were sudden gods,
not waiting for you,
quick decisions in the light,
made to wash the stones
and to make them shine, arise.

But we are here to tell you
that you must wait
for your own thick skull to open,
your own heart to change;

you must wait for words
to leave you,
for your children to die,
for earth, sea, sky,
rivers, horses, olive trees,
to stop their quarrel.

Even if it all
comes apart, limb by limb,
in an easy routine,
and there is no sanctuary
from the flaming, indifferent sky—
that is your burden,
you must still wait.

Lacking prophets,
it is all that we have ever said:
"Just turn the corner
after Egypt, after death

wrapped in the dryness
of the world,

and wait for yourselves—
as long as it takes,
no matter what the stones do,
despite what they do
in the meantime."

ISAAC ON THE *ALTIPLANO*

Say there are high *cordilleras* sharp as glass
against a black sky, a country of lost cities
with the ghosts of children playing on the slopes
of the shining day, places where air is as thin
as a knife blade and breath is locked in stone.

Down below, it is holiday time, with dancers
in flower hats and shawls, women clapping hands,
and men playing flutes; there is *chicha*, too,
the smack of it, along with the graceful prows
of bundle-reed boats on the waters of the Great Lake.

Isaac waits, having come ahead of his father,
impatient to hear the sound of the wind.
Isaac hates the damp cellar of the Andes,
the cobbled keep of the mines; like his father,
he hates the *Aymara* villages, with their bent backs
against the stiff sides of impossible peaks. . . .

And now the sky is near enough to touch;
he turns to watch the old man struggle up behind him
much too slowly, a bird entering darkness
too heavy for wings or the lift of song.

"Here I am," he says to his stiff-legged father,
a pale and brittle figure gasping for breath.

   Isaac kneels to be blessed; he laughs
while the gods, like butterflies, converge on the spot,
   their yellow wings beating like slow hearts,
their empty veins drinking his love.

MIRIAM'S AFTERTHOUGHT

*"So Moses went down from the mountain to the people,
and consecrated the people; and they washed their garments.
And he said to the people, 'Be ready by the third day;
do not go near a woman.' "*
—Exodus 19:14-15

We were caught between two songs,
two kinds of singing, in that
tricky light of morning,
when you dropped down from the mountain
after so long, so full of glory,
free of the senses and free of us.

Nor would we ever know at first hand
what had come down from the sky,
insisting on obedience,
but sowing our bodies with the seeds
of a purity so strict
that we, too, would shine forever.

It was the telling that kept us
bound to it. We heard it
by report, trusting in your wisdom,
that slow choice of words
that took us later, like an embrace
distributed among many.

And what we heard included us,
insisting on us, too,
through a veil of phrases and partial
meanings. Or so we believe,

willing, for a while, to keep
to our tents under the clear dictate
of your rules, among the hills
chosen for your praise.

SAINT BERNARD OF CLAIRVAUX

*"The Holy See prevailed on Bernard to preach the Second
Crusade throughout Europe. His eloquence was so
overwhelming that a great army was assembled and the success
of the crusade seemed assured . . . . [But] the project ended as
a complete disaster."*
— from *Saint of the Day*

In the Cistercian cloister
at Fontenay, the monks gaze up
at darkness fixed at shoulder-height;
only the rise and set
of what is present but unnamed
illuminates the pavement, whose stones
are melody, the work of God,
whose walk is song.

Saint Bernard loved such vaulted shade as this—
these stunted columns
bore the weight of other sounds,
a dark and silent chalice
in the ear of light.

At Cluny, too, the lamb distracted him—
its bleat was wealth
and dignity, embellishment
of crucifix with property;
even the stars were shining disks,
distracting fires struck
on patens, cups, and screens,
jewels on plates of serpentine.

Only in such a carved wilderness
as this, in damp marshes,
on cloudy mountaintops,
could he turn and weep for light.

"I am," he cried, "neither cleric nor layman."

A doubleness to himself,
a mine still deeper into depths,
"I love that I may love," he said, too late.

Then he gave the cross to go,
a medicine to heal the flesh,
to Edessa and to Syria, for love,
to die on burning ground.

THE MAGIC KINGDOM

Coral steeples glow, spiral arms blaze,
and fish leap to the surface; in the branches
of the shade elm, fallen long ago,
but standing exactly where she sees it,

wet leaves shine in the August night;
on the slide down to the final spin,
a voice enters the voice of the rain
on the roof and broken gutters dripping.

Her eyes and ears still stopped in fear,
a thousand years of ghettos and cathedrals
shut behind her like iron gates at dusk,
she discovers a new arrangement of laws—

now the shallow objects of the possible,
the red lion and the white elephant,
all creatures deep and high and tropical,
turn without lingering in soft light.

And, look, she says, arriving at last,
her damaged wings fluttering to a stop,
they pass me by, bearing their riders
out of derangement and shadow forever.

IN A CEMETERY OF THE BIALYSTOK DISTRICT

"What is it then between us?"
—Whitman, "Crossing Brooklyn Ferry"

According to superstition, there are three distinct
apparitions, one of which leaves the body immediately,
   one of which remains with it for a year, and one
of which never leaves it at all. Worship continues
   as before, lights still flicker about the headstones,
and the dead, who stay on, carry on the service,
   observe the holidays, and discuss the commentaries,
just as they did while alive. In their prayers, it is said,
   they struggle to forget themselves and those whom
they need, contending, as in life, against distraction
   and the desires that bewilder and divide them.

At this abandoned cemetery near Bialystok, I like
to think of the death of the dead in this way,
   as if heaven were still the goal of each corpse,
as if each soul (or part of it, as the old wives' tale goes)
   still stood somewhere between addresses, one of them
catacomb or tomb-cave or field of headstones
   and the other beyond the world, yet still the object
of its hope. So that here, among these broken
   and trampled monuments, the dead still struggle
to prevail, remain active and partial. I think of them
   as shadows beyond the inner edge of a painting
left unfinished by a master whose brush stopped exactly
   at the line where nothing and the particular met.

And down the road, in a small village as remote
from the wider world as the dead are from our ever

13

truly knowing them, I listen to the sounds of motors
and horse-drawn carts on the street and watch
  a dark-suited procession leave a church. I imagine
regiments of a romantic vision, of pilgrimage
  and destiny, marching here—ranks of awakening
and revolution, of longing from exile and prison
  in foreign cities. Those were spirit-kings, too,
as the old poems tell us, embodiments of desire,
  harvests of the land, surplus of the soul. They, too,
tramp along this mud-filled road, burn torches
  from far away to lead this village out of suffering
and oppression—the uncollected light of Byron
  and Goethe shining from Carpathia to the Baltic,
from Warsaw to Lublin, from every district and commune,
  where today their own ghosts still wait, lined up
like box cars at a siding of the supernatural.

But where are the final cemeteries of the dead,
forced from this village or lifted on easy winds,
  on seed wings, to another soil? In what dark hold
do they cramp while the engine of the crossing
  carries them away? Along what empty rail lines
do they speed, down clear tracks, to a frontier's edge;
  from what harbor do they sail, cut, like diamonds,
for a new setting? Hell-bent for answers, I try
  turning the corner of such questions. At a table
of friends curious about America, I think of rivers
  and prairies, of ferries and the expanse of bays
that become oceans that then become the one face
  of everything I know and everything I do not know
about where I have been and where I, too, am traveling,
  in pieces and parts, from one place to another.

In the meantime, the seasons, like the wooden churches
and synagogues of Poland, go their own way, pass
    like headstones whose script is chiseled, for a moment,
into everything. Here are castles of the spirit,
    villages waiting for what is to come, unreadable
fragments in scored limestone and melted letters.
    Here, too, are the voices of the birds who cannot ever
mispronounce the accents of this district's past,
    the scale of its suffering, or the measure of its lives.
"Stay here," they seem to say. "Learn how to listen,
    if you can, with at least part of your soul. Stay here,
until you know where the rest of you is going."

THREE FIGURES IN THE LANDSCAPE

i. Moses Maimonides

While the prophets dreamed of chariots
and angels (always dreaming, he said,
the true landscape), his mind grew
like the shoots and tendrils of a vine;

others saw visions or plainly knew
what trailed from the fringes of garments,
fell down from heaven like stars;
some spoke with messengers, unafraid;

but he kept his stark eye on words
that were neither red, green, nor blue,
among meanings that shifted like clouds
across the figureless carpet of sight.

Once, escaping Cordoba, sailing to Acco,
fleeing from Spain and its madness,
a storm nearly wrecked him, the high
sensual seas almost took him down;

he never forgot that almost-touch
of the sky, those mountains of waves
that rose and roared like a woman,
jumped like chaff in the sifter.

Still, he cleared his mind of the chaos,
its systole of reason, its reflex
and diastole of fear. He saw that each
of the attributes, thirteen in all,

of God is mercy. This occurred
as he wrote, exhausted by lamplight,
straining the husks. And the world,
winged like a bird whose body is thought,

took flight. In the dry harbor
of Fostat, a three-hour ride from Cairo,
after medical service to caliph and harem,
he salvaged the sleepless nights—

it was then that the single
and seamless body of the prophets
(whose inflamed flesh was dreams) lay open,
tossing the soul and its laws.

17

ii. Baruch Spinoza

Like the small boat under the bridge
in Rembrandt's painting of the landscape
near Ouderkerk, he passes, in his mind,
through the moment, set apart,

in his loneliness, from the heaviness
of the clouds. This is the sky under which
he lives, into which the tiny church
spire at the lower right barely reaches.

There are no secrets here, but the light
is ominous, full of swirl and sense;
still, he loves solitude and keeps to himself
in the low space framed by the arch

that seems flattened by the weight
of the darkened air. It is hard to believe
how simple this landscape really is,
how logically the fear of smallness

imprints itself on our minds, and how
our limited knowledge of the clouds'
motion across the countryside shatters
our belief in ourselves. But this idea

also sets him apart, lifts him
from the small frame of his boundaries
to a place among mysteries. He is happy
in the language of priests to say so,

though he is not one of them,
and will never be, and the landscape,
in its straightforwardness, its immediate
details, reveals why. He is the child

of the infinite plodding present,
of farmhouse and river and partial light
that never dies, and the beauty
of it all exalts him beyond himself—

to a sharp and meticulous passion
that shapes and grinds him like a blank,
edges him to a spectral fineness,
to an optic of hard and refractory sight.

iii. Martin Buber

"Jewish Villagers Greeting the Messiah,"
by David Kirszenbaum (1900–1953)

The people gathered at the station
are here for an event which is their intention;
scholars, tradesmen, and mothers with children
line the field for the great reception;

a few hold up signs that tell who they are,
readers of psalms, disciples of the rabbi of Kotsk.
But everyone is here, none are absent;
the whole shtetl has come out to meet him.

This is the moment when all waiting ends—
all faces, smiling, lit by the moment,
the light of the hour when all hours pass,
turn toward a figure now fully present.

On a small donkey the rider appears,
his saddlebag stuffed with commandments—
he appears as expected and fills all eyes
while morning light and green pasture

frame the horizon, while cattle graze
indifferently and the station-master watches,
while time stops at the heart of the world
that dissolves with this greeting.

But say that the rider does not appear,
that these voiceless souls, bitter forms,

are unable to speak, that time traps them
in the strict pale of themselves—

the tired villagers slowly disperse,
rabbi, butcher, and beggar jostle in the lanes,
housewife and grocer sadly turn back
toward the market, resume their routines,

managing their midweek business.
Now there are only useful possibilities left
and the dreary landscape continues;
now the blank sun blazes and rails tick

while a vague steam throat sounds
in the distance to tell what approaches
across steppes that extend in all directions,
that join here, that end nowhere.

II. A Vaudeville of the Heart

"It doesn't matter how serious the story
is—it all amounts to a bit of business
or a gag. In the end, everything is a gag."
—Charles Chaplin

"Oh you . . . Something, you Something
because of whom there is not Nothing."
—Saul Bellow

THE LAUGHING MONKEYS OF GRAVITY

i. "The Settlement"

Oliver's pratfall

All bricks must fall on Oliver Hardy's head,
and the imperishable storm do harm to Lear;
Isaac must live to know his place in his father's heart;
let him see how it stood when the knife was out.

Let it all now come to a settlement—
after so long, things should be final and true,
like the hard pavement of Cordelia's lips
or the infallible timing of God's angels.

Just look, for example, at Oliver Hardy—
he's still sitting there on the shattered hearth
while the laughing monkeys of gravity drop
brick after brick on his too-soft head.

Where's his good friend Stanley, his pal?
Right now he's elsewhere, anywhere but where
bricks are falling and the world puts dents
in the skull of someone he loves more than himself.

The monkeys and the angels keep playing,
but Hardy doesn't move—he stares into himself,
waiting for the laughter to stop, furious
at Stanley, unable to think of anyone else.

ii. "The Angel of Light"

Oliver Hardy alone

Sometimes it slips in through curtains
like a needle through the comfort of gauze,
sometimes with a brilliant song and dance;
there are days when it enters like a spine

or a hook through the eye, and I don't know
whether to pull it out or leave it in. Sometimes
it flows down the wall to the baseboard
and spreads itself on the floor like a pool

of honey; that's when I want to swallow it,
to feel it shine from the insides of my cells.
There are days when it doesn't show up
at all, or it hides somewhere in the mirror,

or it hangs, crushed and stale, in the closet,
like an old coat I haven't worn in years.
Each day it's something different, invisible
but seen, a face I know or a sleeping form

at my side, a question I meant to ask
or an unavoidable answer, a familiar visitor,
with or without wings, entering the world,
where I wait for it, not knowing its name.

iii. "The Closed Throat"

the circus mimes

They sit silently in the front parlor
or go from house to house on empty streets
in the dead of night with secrets they promise
to share if I, too, join them for a game

of gestures. I enter their presence
willing to learn their language, their tact,
acting out questions drawn from a hat
about how the dead can leave on a clear

April morning, carried away by a breeze,
while stark sunlight edges the purple hearts
of tulips, puts the pale-white pearl song
in the closed throat of the larkspur.

Then we mime how the knife can enter
when its place arrives and how invisible wires
can guide light down to where it suddenly
darkens itself at the height of its shine;

as if this were still the original time—
world before alphabet, syllable, or sound—
we imitate questions in pancake white-face,
speaking the voices of things as they are.

iv. "Dancing Out, Dancing Back"

Lou Costello (d.1959)

He wakes, he waves his hand and laughs,
dances out, dances back, laughs at nothing,
at some dream he had of dying, as if dying
were just a soft cream pie in the face,

a slip on a banana peel, a circus pen full
of lions seen from the outside. Nothing's hidden,
not even the whirlwind on a bright day
or the reason why keys slip out through bars,

all friends are elsewhere at the moment,
the world seems more beautiful than ever
in that moment of panic. Then he remembers
his useless tears; he recalls how the face

of the sky went dark and turned away;
he sees the exquisite world moving off,
shutting him out of everything he loves,
leaving him behind, to die in lions' jaws.

Dancing out, dancing back, he repeats
this dream to himself, to no one in particular:
that death (he claims) is a song on a page,
a missing key, an absent friend, a cage.

v. "Second-reel Stuff"

Astaire, Gleason, Kaye (d.1987)

As makeshift as a simple fountain pen
jammed quickly into the guts of a broken machine
at the instant everything's on the line
and a hero has to see more than the world;

as lunatic as love in a rage, pointing
a futile finger at fate, hopelessly domestic
in every way; as false as studio snow,
all that interminable talk, the build-up

between numbers and whatever must happen
between two willing lovers—these comedians,
these actors in their parts, were as casual
as death is, too, in its frequent encounters

with clumsiness, with everyday pratfalls,
with whatever makes this the only place
for second-reel stuff. Look how each of them
sidesteps elegy with flawless timing—

as if nothing so final could surpass
the rising action, the perfect performance
of the imperfect about to happen, the random
life of accident, exact and unforeseen.

vi. "In the World's Machine"

Charles Chaplin (d.1977)

While others obey rope and authority,
he breaks free and catches a glimpse of the harbor;
he takes his share, and more, of eyesight,
space, and liberty. He invents his part

in the scheming vaudeville of his heart,
skirts the edge, not seeing it, ignores the book
of credit and debit about to open up,
the moment of truth when the big waiter

raises his eyebrows and flexes his muscles.
But now, trapped at last in the world's machine,
all boundaries and barricades lock him in;
no conflict between dignity and desire

stirs him, no bulk of fat policemen
stops him temporarily or pack of monkeys
on a high wire makes him hesitate in midair;
he's finally down, unable to scramble.

Now love's heavy foot hits the floor,
the wagons roll, and the iris circles shut.
What sockets are there, what blindfold sight
to see with, in worlds beyond the road?

vii. "Oracles of Lefts and Rights"

the Three Stooges

How they stand with those they love
in the houses of closets and mirrors,
but how they fear only what deserves fear:
ghosts, bullies, gangsters, judges, cops,

monsters, shadows, and politicians;
how they hide in corridors while the obscure
and terrible approaches in hobnail boots
with its dire intentions; how they know

nothing at all, or just enough to keep
clear of learning, callings, and degrees;
how, lacking skills, practice, or profession,
they understand those oracles of lefts

and rights to the head from all angles
that tell them who they are and where they are,
but never why; how they somehow survive
without the least speculation or thought.

And how, afterwards—late afternoons
beyond an exit, slow drizzle on pavement,
the unhappy way home—the three of them
stay behind, better off in the dark.

31

viii. "The Snowmen"

Keaton (d.1966) and Lloyd (d.1971)

And now we know it's time to lay
our sleepy heads down on steel tracks,
ride the cow-catcher into space,
hang from time's nightmare hands;

we'll swan-dive into tall haystacks
soft as down, hide in the magic box,
a backstage prop, while swords probe
for our bellies. Despite what we know

about how empty the darkness really is,
we'll wait down by the icy stream
in the hollow, near the fallen picket fence,
for our fat old friends to appear.

And when they come, with their scarves
and carrot noses, their dripping bodies,
"Hurry," they'll say, feeling the thaw,
impatient to play before they dissolve.

After a while, we'll fall to earth
—parachutes opening just in time—
to find cops everywhere, blue flowers
on the run, chasing us through spring.

ix. "Empty Rooms"

Oliver Hardy (d.1957)

But mouths still open in dark mirrors,
eyes watch in empty rooms; nothing moves
but the half-light on a screen, nothing stirs
but fictions in a stall between reels.

Now Oliver Hardy, dead many years,
himself once a teller of tales, as pure
a lover of laughter as there ever was,
shifts in his armchair, wakes from his nap.

I hauled that chair from a thousand miles away,
with its crushed pile, its sagging springs,
kept it for him. Now he looks around,
wondering where he is, the road in his eyes,

city, countryside, shore in his head,
long summer days on the move with Stan.
"All that clutter!" he suddenly whispers,
trying to make sense of my house.

Oliver Hardy fixes me with his gaze:
"I see you think you know me," he says.
"Better put some coffee on," he adds.
And then: "I think we need to talk."

x. "Missed Connection"

Stan Laurel (d. 1965)

Now, at last, everything's down, or in,
lives through which we've traveled to reach
this place, suddenly-remembered itineraries,
flights in harvest moon, through clouds.

This might be a terminal in Fort Smith,
the next bus hours off in the gray dawn;
it might be an airport motel between flights,
an unscheduled stop, our baggage lost,

all possible destinations out of reach,
a missed connection, the world a fat man's
brown mudhole on another rainy night.
More still, more alone than ever, we wait.

In the flickering light, Hardy and I wait
while shadows of angels dance overhead;
we wait for the last sharp brick to fall,
remembering Stanley, our friend, our pal.

The laughing monkeys tumble and roar
while Oliver Hardy collects himself;
he seats himself on the first flight out,
at home, unmoved, wherever he rides.

III. Songs and Voices

"Just as my fingers on these keys
Make music, so the self-same sounds
On my spirit make a music, too."
                    —Wallace Stevens

"Every one of his song compositions
is in reality a poem on the poem he set
to music . . ."
                    —Joseph von Spaun,
                    Recollections of Schubert

FIRST VOICES

We have a few of their voices, Enrico Caruso's
most important of all, but there were others:
Luisa Tetrazzini's, for example, as Gilda,
recorded in 1911. Why do they move us more
than any present sense of who's in the room
with us tonight, or will be, soon enough,
for the usual pleasant talk, for an hour or so?
Is it because theirs are voices never heard before,
coins never counted, paintings never seen,
stone ships on the waves of a watery world,
and we are the last to have known them, the last
to recall the first of the speaking dead?
At least we think there were visits during
which we drank tea, sliced bread on enameled
tabletops; we listened to stories, too,
on sofas with cushions in needlepoint before
fading away into other registers. Not much else
that hasn't slipped away from the easy
hearing of the present, where our children's
children play among their own unfelt sounds.
In the empty houses of the immediate, we try
to entertain them with our natural voices,
small relics of attention, ghosts of bread
and butter, tidbits, we hope, of useful talk.

Say it's snowing on 57th Street on a particular
morning in February, 1904. In a studio
in Carnegie Hall, Caruso is singing an aria
of Donizetti's; he draws out several passages,
and a decision is made to cut two discs,
rather than one. Meanwhile, outside, someone

we once knew, or think we did, boards a trolley
going downtown on Seventh Avenue. Thinking
of nothing at the moment, he watches the curb,
while, at the same time, across the street,
the engineer from Victor Gramophone notes the place
where the second disc starts. *Un solo istante,*
Caruso sings, an event in wax, an entry in the sum
of all sounds otherwise made but lost. Tonight
we listen to that *mezzo-voce* as if it were
the last of our flat and scratchy connections
on the turning surface of an old and brittle planet.

"BEETHOVEN DOES NOT LIE HERE"

Franz Schubert's last words

Mornings when he wrote, his hand flawless
across the page, the night's chat at Bogner's Cafe
    or the Anchor Tavern yawned like sleep into the wide sky;
Vienna danced and sang; the brass bands in the Prater,

    the organ-grinders, signed themselves in voices.
Like the deaf master whom he loved, he raised
    the dark indefinite body of sound up from its bones,
its triple-flesh, finishing what Goethe and Schiller

    had only begun, turning flat speech, stiff
tropes, and inadequate rhymes into the poems of poems.
    Alpine scores ran through his brain, evenings
of generous accompaniment, and improvised waltzes, too;

    he saw wildflowers dance on a paper field;
carriages crossed the green of his eye; high clouds
    bunched in the heavy skies; the chill November rain
still held his quick flammable ear to the flame.

A GARLAND FOR SKELTON

John Skelton, rude railing rhymster,
mad with the itch, the ropey rain,
the roast pig's ear of terms and matter,
skilled in graceful turns of Latin,
imagines his finished Book of Works—
this book, he says, with gold mosaic
in every other line is written;
its margins are full of bees and wasps,
of butterflies and peacock tails.
Flowers and slimy snails all garnish
the style and its effect, which is,
he claims, a natural music that rolls
from plain green English into life.
Elinour Rumming and her tunning of ale
are here and elegist Jane Scroop,
Philip Sparrow's mistress, and Wolsey,
lunatic with power. And in a dream,
as Skelton lay at Harwich Port,
are nightmare Hafter, Favel, and Dawes,
cargo of epithet, ship of court.
Here are birds, too, of every kind,
a cuckoo-watch of learning, morning's
wake of rhyme and tumbling stanza,
a feathered choir-nest of heaven.
Yet wickedness is everywhere,
and friars fall into wells and cannot,
for holiness, sing themselves out
without the help of Colin Clout.

At the edge of bristling singsong
the jawed line jetties into bays;

Skelton, who praised his bastard child
before the scandalized folk at Diss,
could not stop at couplets' ends
or point in meter like hard brick.
Horatian clerks, in whose conceit
Magnyfycence became Augustus,
halted on lame and proper feet;
but Skelton put sunlight into lines
that rage against ungodly cloth
and laugh with folk in tavern talk;
doggerel, his muddy rivals say,
whose craft is tame and neat to his.

BEWILDERING CLARITY OF TONGUES

for Aaron Lebedeff (1873-1960),
performer on the Yiddish stage

Bewildering clarity of tongues:
names you never heard, food
you never ate, a wild dance
you never learned, light hanging
in the sky like a blue dish
for a special occasion . . .

His voice reminded you of a peddler's
cry at the penny in your hand.
A few of the old-timers told you
about him; they'd seen him perform
on the Lower East Side. But something
still came between what they said
and the music, like pavement

between your feet and the cobblestones
underneath. Then you imagined
all the pennies you'd ever seen,
gathering them up in a pushcart of your own
and taking them down to a market
where men with dripping noses
and women in greasy aprons
sold their goods in the stalls.

"I will sell you a voice you can recognize,"
one of them said. "It will fill
your room at night with shining forms."

"I will sell you a voice
you cannot recognize," said another.
"All you will know is your need."

But a third cried out, "What's best
for you are voices that sing
like the shine of stars behind a thick
curtain of stars. Here are clouts
of light from the three-wheeled urn
of night, and these remnants
are the only ones worth having."

And that was what you bought:
voice through a double-brick wall,
echo in the air shaft of the day,
music that ran on the rails
of your body and entered its cells
like stations, all you would ever know
of a dance in the next room.

43

THOMSON'S GAZELLE

speed, along with circuits
for escape, elusiveness

in the open field, sure hoofs
for sidetracking, a torso

that can change direction
midair, lyrate horns, coat

with coloring the color
of horizon on the open plain,

along with judgment
quick enough to know danger

an instant before it strikes
from the tall grass

that edges the way to water—
but not useless imagination,

not innocence, not one question
out of its windpipe

that a child might ask,
or a poet move his slow tongue

to answer, unless the sky, too,
were locked in his throat.

WHEN I CAME TO HEAVEN

for Mani Leib (1883–1953), poet,
cobbler, man of many trades

Singing,
I was the last to walk
in the dry flowerbeds
of my cells,

the first to float
to the shore
of the world's edge,

the last to dream,
the first to live.

I was the first to wake,
hearing the green waves

sing their name,
which was mine, also.

But even then,
I was the first to remember

the lonely houses
of the familiar,

the last to sing farewell
to all my dead kin,

while the sky still
shattered overhead.

I was the first
to wear a crown among
lilies and roses,

but the last
to blossom at the bone.

When I came to heaven,
called to my vocation,
I was the first
to return to my limbs,

safe from all conclusions,

still singing.

ANNIVERSARY SONG

Someone's at the door, a surprise.

She has green eyes.

Another afternoon
on its way into history,
another surprising afternoon:

the letters of Van Gogh,
a book about the Third Reich,
put aside,

along with something I'd begun,
half-finished, all sweat,
not one line of truth,

nothing I wouldn't
give up or haven't already given up,
to have this, right now.

What I have is
that bird's nest fern
beside the rocker, cut
irises in the blue swirl vase,

and this company.

Let the music take care of itself.

This is what I have.

47

This is what I want.

I do, I keep saying,
I do, I do.

A CIRCUMSTANCE OF THE PORCH

You're in your robe and slippers,
and it's just the Sunday paper
you want, when someone saying he's

your father suddenly slides out
from behind the wheel of a blue
late-model wagon and a woman

calling herself mother waves
from the passenger's side, too
happy to move. The two of them

start unloading bags, gifts, food,
a set of electric trains,
a box of your old toy soldiers.

You can feel the shine coming back
to your face, hear white steeples,
crystal sets, the cheerful man

in the tube talking, the announcer
bringing on comedians or singers
or this week's mystery-installment.

It's a circumstance of the porch.
Say hello. Start talking. Smile.
You've waited all week for this.

SPEAKING OF COUSINS

From her penthouse window, after lunch,
my well-married cousin looks down
at the Queensboro Bridge with the eye
of a fine arts major who can buy anything
she wants but, for her own reasons,
has decided not to make the purchase.

It's our first meeting in years,
and I remind her how, once, as children,
in a skipjack, with her father at the helm,
we rode out a storm on Long Beach Bay,
but she doesn't recall the adventure.
The visit soon ends, an entry in two
busy calendars, a length of string
in a box I sometimes open up, labeled
"Loose ends, to be tied up later."

A day later, I'm stopping with friends
in the country, looking at albums
of kinfolk and kinfolk-neighbors.
Afterwards we go upstairs to tour
old bed frames, chairs, tables, toys,
a jumble like the last set of *Citizen Kane*
crammed into one farmhouse attic
somewhere in empty New Hampshire.

After the heirlooms, it's time for lunch,
for chowder, fries, and frappes;
it's also time to be speaking of cousins
and then to greet them as they arrive,

one after another, in the middle
of nowhere, at a county fair of kin.

It's a circumstance like worn linoleum
or fallen fences, but needing to be blessed;
it evokes admiration, like the appearance
of an empty table at the busiest hour
of the day, no need for reservations.

Wearing blue-twill work clothes
in a country grill in Yankee limbo
or exquisite pearls and silk casuals
in a crowded pub at ground zero,
cousins hiss like damp wood in the fire,
pull the light-chains in our dark heads,
keep the rockers going in the attic.

THE UNCLES

i.

They were all there for a while,
even the great gorilla, fur-draped blonde
in hand, and the howling mob, all,
joined together in the fire.

They were all there on family-Sundays,
the ones in baggy trousers with smiles,
the ones in broad-brimmed hats;
Spade was there, Captain Bligh,
and Captain Blood; couples tripped,
then flickered through the frame,
picking themselves up after each fall
(the light was not to blame).

Vaughn was there, in full voice,
and Bix, triple-tongued, and others,
dancing or watching, charmed,
and Groucho, Chico, and Harpo,
before the curtain dropped
and the high-key houselights went out,
in the middle of a scene
they all meant to steal forever.

ii.

In the steerage of the house,
there were dishes for holiday meals
and landscapes hung from the planking;
there were books and letters
brought here from long ago.

There were tools down there, too,
and the oldest uncle, the fixer,
the joiner and mender of fragments,
keeping busy at his workbench;
his bright face went out, went blank,
in the noisy rooms upstairs.

Among beams of earth and root,
in the narrow shaded yard,
he coaxed sunlight to fall exactly
where he wanted it to, with his
delicate long-handled hoe.

His flowers stood like judgments against the eye,
the wide fish eye of light;
the light ran, laughing-sliding down chutes,
into the coal bin of his arms.

iii.

But right now, tonight,
the very last of them has left,
gone to a time and a place
I cannot ever remember or reconstruct,
setting him against a dark piano,
stuccoed walls, and flowers in a bowl.

And if I'm right, there'll be
no other satin table in the corner
under portraits, grayer heads than his,
clutter of the heart there, either,
or blossoms pressed flat between pages
in journals for him to show,
to be read only with fingertips,
in the thick dark that eats up his eyes.

Tonight, after so many uncles,
the house is crowded again with visitors,
with relatives unseen for years;
a gravity of kin draws us all in
to these shroud-mirrored rooms,
one last time, before we scatter.

HER SUDDEN DEATH

Hats, pins, plates, vases,
rings, mirrors, broken watches,
linen, ladles, and shoes
must all, suddenly, be spoken for.
And we, who document her life,
the red incineration of her life,
must now account for them,
while outside in the hallway closet
neighbors dump their trash.

All around us fish swim
in the balanced flight of sleep,
the flying darkness of dreams,
clanking heaters warm
drafty senior housing rooms,
spools of yarn and leftover patterns
collect in heaps. The short day
declares its frigid winter notice
of what all strangers share,
muffled in their small apartments,
fixing meals in tiny kitchens,
cornered by their white appliances.

Dresses, gowns, and prints,
perfume, beads, old checks, and keys—
for now these few loose ends concern us,
these rag-tag matters hold us.
Just half in, half out of our eyes,
her passing found us unprepared
to wake this house with cries
of grief to empty skies.

THREE ANATOMISTS

i.

Leonardo himself warns us of a certain loathing
or fear in the night hours of the company of corpses,
quartered and flayed and horrible to see. He adds
that skill in drawing is a requirement, a sense

of perspective, an understanding of geometry,
a knowledge of how to calculate forces; patience, also,
since one body does not last so long. He himself
examined ten bodies, proceeding by degrees,

to come, as he says, to his goal, which was nothing less
than true knowledge. He wanted, he said, to work
miracles, by which he meant those acts of knowing
that reach us through direct experience and become

possessions of the soul. He set out first to discard
authority, then to examine for himself rocks,
soil, air, mountains, water, the flight of birds,
the play of light and shadow, things already seen

but unknown to those who had merely studied images.
So we find him by candlelight, working miracles,
dissecting members, viscera, exposing articulations,
considering the wonderful planes of the body, its

positions and torsions of pronation and supination,
noting colors and complexions, the flax-like skein
of nerve-in-muscle that, under running water,
clings and unites, making it impossible to trace

in all of its ramifications. In semi-darkness
he did fifteen drawings: the cosmography, he hoped,
when finished, of this lesser world and counterpart
of Ptolemy's glorious plan of the greater one.

ii.

In his feverish illness, Descartes looked out
at the countryside, at the rain, and felt once again
his need for warmth, his dizziness after height,
his loneliness after stiff ritual. He dreamed

he woke up one morning outside himself, in a place
he'd never been. He saw himself disconnected,
apart from motion and sense—a floating point
in the gap between earth and sky. The heavy snow

covered the fields that winter while he slept
and took his meals in a well-heated room;
the dreary town of Neuberg offered no distractions
while he reinvented space. But his nightmare continued—

it was the end of thinking, grief in the house,
the hard frost outside, and the thick brown earth
always finishing what was said. At the corner
of ceiling and walls, he saw death flap its wings;

he heard sounds rushing through the dark house,
weeping in the empty corridor. Afterwards, he needed
still more warmth, the gift of pure consolation,
the sheltering body itself to come and sleep with him,

a place to rest from thought. It was then that he knew
what had spoken first, asked the first questions—
in the cold dawn of St. Martin's Day, he pulled
his blankets around him and closed his eyes.

He saw in his fever the only place in which
he'd ever be: the name of the stars and his pulse,
the only map at the one intersection of all
other maps, the one continent of all his parts.

iii.

In the expressionless face of child or friend,
the final instant of its structure, Emily Dickinson
considered its elegant plan. The body, too,
practiced silence in tight arrangements, statement

in the precise symmetries of its still details.
In the strings and wires of its fibers, its voice
was as spare as the simplest hymn; in the coda
of its rigorous end, there were few flourishes.

She considered, as well, the minute particulars
of her own life: its taut economies of gesture,
its constant course from day to day. She thought, too,
about what an eternity might be: a faint smear

in granite, the smell of rich garden dirt
under her fingernails, kitchen steam on a winter window,
the loud crack of summer thunder over the house
in which she lived. Under her father's roof

or on the nearby common, such distinctions
of form and time, of heaven and ground, seemed
to meet in points of sense. In the mid-March light,
scored by branches, she looked again at the mask

and considered what it was, and, as she did,
heard the sounds beyond the window of carriages
and belfry, of slow iron-rimmed wheels
going forward through a sky of fresh puddles;

she saw the anterior and posterior divisions,
the union of the divisions, the crosshatching
of gray sky and tiny white clusters, late-winter
anemones under the pale shadows of birds.

GEORGIA FREEZE

When the pipes burst in three hundred places
and all the other late additions failed the truth
that entered with the freeze, every plant died
but the cactus and paint peeled off the walls
of the antebellum house built to keep out summer.

There were arms, legs, and heads everywhere;
the night sounds of the train yard slipped in
through cracked panes; there were angry voices
in the wide entrance hall, where the first guests
had arrived long ago, seeking the cool.

It was our title, though not our house, as yet;
sooner or later, we hoped, warm sunlight
might return through the clerestory windows
set to the east and north, the first thaw enter,
like a welcome guest, stamping its feet;
in the meantime, the house held the freeze
between its joists, under its floor boards,
in its cast-iron mantles and blue-tile facings.

After a while, we inspected the parlor;
we saw how the seamless wide pine flooring
and the curved wall would make a setting
for the yellow sofa with the flower pattern;
we saw how the lamp with the fluted shade
would stand beside the sofa, in the corner.
We saw many combinations, all possible.

Strangers from elsewhere, new arrivals,
we saw that our ideas would have to wait
while we gave it a chance to think us over,
while we settled our differences one by one,
earned our welcome, in slow, sweet time.